REPERTOIRE LOG

No.	Title

REPERTOIRE LOG

No.	Title

PRACTICE LOG

Lesson/Start Date(s):

Practice Goal: (MINS/DAY)

*SCALES, CHORDS, ARPEGGIOS, MUSIC PIECES, THEORY, PAGE NO. ETC...

✓ / Minutes / Signature etc. . .

CATEGORY*	NOTES	Su	Mo	Tu	We	Th	Fr	Sa

Lesson/Start Date(s):

Practice Goal: (MINS/DAY)

*SCALES, CHORDS, ARPEGGIOS, MUSIC PIECES, THEORY, PAGE NO. ETC...

✓ / Minutes / Signature etc. . .

CATEGORY*	NOTES	Su	Mo	Tu	We	Th	Fr	Sa

ADDITIONAL NOTES:

PRACTICE LOG

Lesson/Start Date(s): _____ *Practice Goal: (MINS/DAY)* _____

SCALES, CHORDS, ARPEGGIOS, MUSIC PIECES, THEORY, PAGE NO. ETC...   ✓ / Minutes / Signature etc...

CATEGORY*	NOTES	Su	Mo	Tu	We	Th	Fr	Sa

Lesson/Start Date(s): _____ *Practice Goal: (MINS/DAY)* _____

SCALES, CHORDS, ARPEGGIOS, MUSIC PIECES, THEORY, PAGE NO. ETC...   ✓ / Minutes / Signature etc...

CATEGORY*	NOTES	Su	Mo	Tu	We	Th	Fr	Sa

ADDITIONAL NOTES:

PRACTICE LOG

Lesson/Start Date(s): _____

Practice Goal: (MINS/DAY) _____

*SCALES, CHORDS, ARPEGGIOS, MUSIC PIECES, THEORY, PAGE NO. ETC...   ✓ / Minutes / Signature etc. . .

CATEGORY*	NOTES	Su	Mo	Tu	We	Th	Fr	Sa

Lesson/Start Date(s): _____

Practice Goal: (MINS/DAY) _____

*SCALES, CHORDS, ARPEGGIOS, MUSIC PIECES, THEORY, PAGE NO. ETC...   ✓ / Minutes / Signature etc. . .

CATEGORY*	NOTES	Su	Mo	Tu	We	Th	Fr	Sa

ADDITIONAL NOTES:

PRACTICE LOG

Lesson/Start Date(s): _____   *Practice Goal:* (MINS/DAY) _____

*SCALES, CHORDS, ARPEGGIOS, MUSIC PIECES, THEORY, PAGE NO. ETC...   ✓ / Minutes / Signature etc...

CATEGORY*	NOTES	Su	Mo	Tu	We	Th	Fr	Sa

Lesson/Start Date(s): _____   *Practice Goal:* (MINS/DAY) _____

*SCALES, CHORDS, ARPEGGIOS, MUSIC PIECES, THEORY, PAGE NO. ETC...   ✓ / Minutes / Signature etc...

CATEGORY*	NOTES	Su	Mo	Tu	We	Th	Fr	Sa

ADDITIONAL NOTES:

PRACTICE LOG

Lesson/Start Date(s):

Practice Goal: (MINS/DAY)

*SCALES, CHORDS, ARPEGGIOS, MUSIC PIECES, THEORY, PAGE NO. ETC...

✓ / Minutes / Signature etc. . .

CATEGORY*	NOTES	Su	Mo	Tu	We	Th	Fr	Sa

Lesson/Start Date(s):

Practice Goal: (MINS/DAY)

*SCALES, CHORDS, ARPEGGIOS, MUSIC PIECES, THEORY, PAGE NO. ETC...

✓ / Minutes / Signature etc. . .

CATEGORY*	NOTES	Su	Mo	Tu	We	Th	Fr	Sa

ADDITIONAL NOTES:

PRACTICE LOG

Lesson/Start Date(s):

Practice Goal: (MINS/DAY)

*SCALES, CHORDS, ARPEGGIOS, MUSIC PIECES, THEORY, PAGE NO. ETC...

✓ / Minutes / Signature etc...

CATEGORY*	NOTES	Su	Mo	Tu	We	Th	Fr	Sa

Lesson/Start Date(s):

Practice Goal: (MINS/DAY)

*SCALES, CHORDS, ARPEGGIOS, MUSIC PIECES, THEORY, PAGE NO. ETC...

✓ / Minutes / Signature etc...

CATEGORY*	NOTES	Su	Mo	Tu	We	Th	Fr	Sa

ADDITIONAL NOTES:

PRACTICE LOG

Lesson/Start Date(s): _____

Practice Goal: (MINS/DAY) _____

*SCALES, CHORDS, ARPEGGIOS, MUSIC PIECES, THEORY, PAGE NO. ETC...

✓ / Minutes / Signature etc...

CATEGORY*	NOTES	Su	Mo	Tu	We	Th	Fr	Sa

Lesson/Start Date(s): _____

Practice Goal: (MINS/DAY) _____

*SCALES, CHORDS, ARPEGGIOS, MUSIC PIECES, THEORY, PAGE NO. ETC...

✓ / Minutes / Signature etc...

CATEGORY*	NOTES	Su	Mo	Tu	We	Th	Fr	Sa

ADDITIONAL NOTES:

PRACTICE LOG

Lesson/Start Date(s):

Practice Goal: (MINS/DAY)

*SCALES, CHORDS, ARPEGGIOS, MUSIC PIECES, THEORY, PAGE NO. ETC...

✓ / Minutes / Signature etc...

CATEGORY*	NOTES	Su	Mo	Tu	We	Th	Fr	Sa

Lesson/Start Date(s):

Practice Goal: (MINS/DAY)

*SCALES, CHORDS, ARPEGGIOS, MUSIC PIECES, THEORY, PAGE NO. ETC...

✓ / Minutes / Signature etc...

CATEGORY*	NOTES	Su	Mo	Tu	We	Th	Fr	Sa

ADDITIONAL NOTES:

PRACTICE LOG

Lesson/Start Date(s):

Practice Goal: (MINS/DAY)

*SCALES, CHORDS, ARPEGGIOS, MUSIC PIECES, THEORY, PAGE NO. ETC...

✓ / Minutes / Signature etc...

CATEGORY*	NOTES	Su	Mo	Tu	We	Th	Fr	Sa

Lesson/Start Date(s):

Practice Goal: (MINS/DAY)

*SCALES, CHORDS, ARPEGGIOS, MUSIC PIECES, THEORY, PAGE NO. ETC...

✓ / Minutes / Signature etc...

CATEGORY*	NOTES	Su	Mo	Tu	We	Th	Fr	Sa

ADDITIONAL NOTES:

PRACTICE LOG

Lesson/Start Date(s):

Practice Goal: (MINS/DAY)

*SCALES, CHORDS, ARPEGGIOS, MUSIC PIECES, THEORY, PAGE NO. ETC...

✓ / Minutes / Signature etc...

CATEGORY*	NOTES	Su	Mo	Tu	We	Th	Fr	Sa

Lesson/Start Date(s):

Practice Goal: (MINS/DAY)

*SCALES, CHORDS, ARPEGGIOS, MUSIC PIECES, THEORY, PAGE NO. ETC...

✓ / Minutes / Signature etc...

CATEGORY*	NOTES	Su	Mo	Tu	We	Th	Fr	Sa

ADDITIONAL NOTES:

PRACTICE LOG

Lesson/Start Date(s):

Practice Goal: (MINS/DAY)

*SCALES, CHORDS, ARPEGGIOS, MUSIC PIECES, THEORY, PAGE NO. ETC...

✓ / Minutes / Signature etc...

CATEGORY*	NOTES	Su	Mo	Tu	We	Th	Fr	Sa

Lesson/Start Date(s):

Practice Goal: (MINS/DAY)

*SCALES, CHORDS, ARPEGGIOS, MUSIC PIECES, THEORY, PAGE NO. ETC...

✓ / Minutes / Signature etc...

CATEGORY*	NOTES	Su	Mo	Tu	We	Th	Fr	Sa

ADDITIONAL NOTES:

PRACTICE LOG

Lesson/Start Date(s): _____

Practice Goal: (MINS/DAY) _____

*SCALES, CHORDS, ARPEGGIOS, MUSIC PIECES, THEORY, PAGE NO. ETC...

✓ / Minutes / Signature etc. . .

CATEGORY*	NOTES	Su	Mo	Tu	We	Th	Fr	Sa

Lesson/Start Date(s): _____

Practice Goal: (MINS/DAY) _____

*SCALES, CHORDS, ARPEGGIOS, MUSIC PIECES, THEORY, PAGE NO. ETC...

✓ / Minutes / Signature etc. . .

CATEGORY*	NOTES	Su	Mo	Tu	We	Th	Fr	Sa

ADDITIONAL NOTES:

PRACTICE LOG

Lesson/Start Date(s):

Practice Goal: (MINS/DAY)

SCALES, CHORDS, ARPEGGIOS, MUSIC PIECES, THEORY, PAGE NO. ETC...   ✓ / Minutes / Signature etc...

CATEGORY*	NOTES	Su	Mo	Tu	We	Th	Fr	Sa

Lesson/Start Date(s):

Practice Goal: (MINS/DAY)

SCALES, CHORDS, ARPEGGIOS, MUSIC PIECES, THEORY, PAGE NO. ETC...   ✓ / Minutes / Signature etc...

CATEGORY*	NOTES	Su	Mo	Tu	We	Th	Fr	Sa

ADDITIONAL NOTES:

PRACTICE LOG

| Lesson/Start Date(s): | | Practice Goal: (MINS/DAY) | |

*SCALES, CHORDS, ARPEGGIOS, MUSIC PIECES, THEORY, PAGE NO. ETC... ✓ / Minutes / Signature etc. . .

CATEGORY*	NOTES	Su	Mo	Tu	We	Th	Fr	Sa

| Lesson/Start Date(s): | | Practice Goal: (MINS/DAY) | |

*SCALES, CHORDS, ARPEGGIOS, MUSIC PIECES, THEORY, PAGE NO. ETC... ✓ / Minutes / Signature etc. . .

CATEGORY*	NOTES	Su	Mo	Tu	We	Th	Fr	Sa

ADDITIONAL NOTES:

PRACTICE LOG

Lesson/Start Date(s):

Practice Goal: (MINS/DAY)

*SCALES, CHORDS, ARPEGGIOS, MUSIC PIECES, THEORY, PAGE NO. ETC...

✓ / Minutes / Signature etc. . .

CATEGORY*	NOTES	Su	Mo	Tu	We	Th	Fr	Sa

Lesson/Start Date(s):

Practice Goal: (MINS/DAY)

*SCALES, CHORDS, ARPEGGIOS, MUSIC PIECES, THEORY, PAGE NO. ETC...

✓ / Minutes / Signature etc. . .

CATEGORY*	NOTES	Su	Mo	Tu	We	Th	Fr	Sa

ADDITIONAL NOTES:

PRACTICE LOG

Lesson/Start Date(s): _____

Practice Goal: (MINS/DAY) _____

*SCALES, CHORDS, ARPEGGIOS, MUSIC PIECES, THEORY, PAGE NO. ETC...

✓ / Minutes / Signature etc. . .

CATEGORY*	NOTES	Su	Mo	Tu	We	Th	Fr	Sa

Lesson/Start Date(s): _____

Practice Goal: (MINS/DAY) _____

*SCALES, CHORDS, ARPEGGIOS, MUSIC PIECES, THEORY, PAGE NO. ETC...

✓ / Minutes / Signature etc. . .

CATEGORY*	NOTES	Su	Mo	Tu	We	Th	Fr	Sa

ADDITIONAL NOTES:

PRACTICE LOG

Lesson/Start Date(s):

Practice Goal: (MINS/DAY)

*SCALES, CHORDS, ARPEGGIOS, MUSIC PIECES, THEORY, PAGE NO. ETC...

✓ / Minutes / Signature etc. . .

CATEGORY*	NOTES	Su	Mo	Tu	We	Th	Fr	Sa

Lesson/Start Date(s):

Practice Goal: (MINS/DAY)

*SCALES, CHORDS, ARPEGGIOS, MUSIC PIECES, THEORY, PAGE NO. ETC...

✓ / Minutes / Signature etc. . .

CATEGORY*	NOTES	Su	Mo	Tu	We	Th	Fr	Sa

ADDITIONAL NOTES:

PRACTICE LOG

Lesson/Start Date(s): _____

Practice Goal: (MINS/DAY) _____

*SCALES, CHORDS, ARPEGGIOS, MUSIC PIECES, THEORY, PAGE NO. ETC...

✓ / Minutes / Signature etc. . .

CATEGORY*	NOTES	Su	Mo	Tu	We	Th	Fr	Sa

Lesson/Start Date(s): _____

Practice Goal: (MINS/DAY) _____

*SCALES, CHORDS, ARPEGGIOS, MUSIC PIECES, THEORY, PAGE NO. ETC...

✓ / Minutes / Signature etc. . .

CATEGORY*	NOTES	Su	Mo	Tu	We	Th	Fr	Sa

ADDITIONAL NOTES:

PRACTICE LOG

Lesson/Start Date(s):

Practice Goal: (MINS/DAY)

*SCALES, CHORDS, ARPEGGIOS, MUSIC PIECES, THEORY, PAGE NO. ETC...

✓ / Minutes / Signature etc. . .

CATEGORY*	NOTES	Su	Mo	Tu	We	Th	Fr	Sa

Lesson/Start Date(s):

Practice Goal: (MINS/DAY)

*SCALES, CHORDS, ARPEGGIOS, MUSIC PIECES, THEORY, PAGE NO. ETC...

✓ / Minutes / Signature etc. . .

CATEGORY*	NOTES	Su	Mo	Tu	We	Th	Fr	Sa

ADDITIONAL NOTES:

PRACTICE LOG

Lesson/Start Date(s): _____

Practice Goal: (MINS/DAY) _____

*SCALES, CHORDS, ARPEGGIOS, MUSIC PIECES, THEORY, PAGE NO. ETC...

✓ / Minutes / Signature etc. . .

CATEGORY*	NOTES	Su	Mo	Tu	We	Th	Fr	Sa

Lesson/Start Date(s): _____

Practice Goal: (MINS/DAY) _____

*SCALES, CHORDS, ARPEGGIOS, MUSIC PIECES, THEORY, PAGE NO. ETC...

✓ / Minutes / Signature etc. . .

CATEGORY*	NOTES	Su	Mo	Tu	We	Th	Fr	Sa

ADDITIONAL NOTES:

PRACTICE LOG

| Lesson/Start Date(s): | | Practice Goal: (MINS/DAY) | |

*SCALES, CHORDS, ARPEGGIOS, MUSIC PIECES, THEORY, PAGE NO. ETC...   ✓ / Minutes / Signature etc...

CATEGORY*	NOTES	Su	Mo	Tu	We	Th	Fr	Sa

| Lesson/Start Date(s): | | Practice Goal: (MINS/DAY) | |

*SCALES, CHORDS, ARPEGGIOS, MUSIC PIECES, THEORY, PAGE NO. ETC...   ✓ / Minutes / Signature etc...

CATEGORY*	NOTES	Su	Mo	Tu	We	Th	Fr	Sa

ADDITIONAL NOTES:

PRACTICE LOG

Lesson/Start Date(s): _____   *Practice Goal: (MINS/DAY)* _____

*SCALES, CHORDS, ARPEGGIOS, MUSIC PIECES, THEORY, PAGE NO. ETC...   ✓ / Minutes / Signature etc. . .

CATEGORY*	NOTES	Su	Mo	Tu	We	Th	Fr	Sa

Lesson/Start Date(s): _____   *Practice Goal: (MINS/DAY)* _____

*SCALES, CHORDS, ARPEGGIOS, MUSIC PIECES, THEORY, PAGE NO. ETC...   ✓ / Minutes / Signature etc. . .

CATEGORY*	NOTES	Su	Mo	Tu	We	Th	Fr	Sa

ADDITIONAL NOTES:

PRACTICE LOG

Lesson/Start Date(s): _____   **Practice Goal: (MINS/DAY)** _____

*SCALES, CHORDS, ARPEGGIOS, MUSIC PIECES, THEORY, PAGE NO. ETC...   ✓ / Minutes / Signature etc...

CATEGORY*	NOTES	Su	Mo	Tu	We	Th	Fr	Sa

Lesson/Start Date(s): _____   **Practice Goal: (MINS/DAY)** _____

*SCALES, CHORDS, ARPEGGIOS, MUSIC PIECES, THEORY, PAGE NO. ETC...   ✓ / Minutes / Signature etc...

CATEGORY*	NOTES	Su	Mo	Tu	We	Th	Fr	Sa

ADDITIONAL NOTES:

PRACTICE LOG

Lesson/Start Date(s): _____

Practice Goal: (MINS/DAY) _____

SCALES, CHORDS, ARPEGGIOS, MUSIC PIECES, THEORY, PAGE NO. ETC...

✓ / Minutes / Signature etc. . .

CATEGORY*	NOTES	Su	Mo	Tu	We	Th	Fr	Sa

Lesson/Start Date(s): _____

Practice Goal: (MINS/DAY) _____

SCALES, CHORDS, ARPEGGIOS, MUSIC PIECES, THEORY, PAGE NO. ETC...

✓ / Minutes / Signature etc. . .

CATEGORY*	NOTES	Su	Mo	Tu	We	Th	Fr	Sa

ADDITIONAL NOTES:

PRACTICE LOG

| Lesson/Start Date(s): | | Practice Goal: (MINS/DAY) | |

*SCALES, CHORDS, ARPEGGIOS, MUSIC PIECES, THEORY, PAGE NO. ETC... ✓ / Minutes / Signature etc...

CATEGORY*	NOTES	Su	Mo	Tu	We	Th	Fr	Sa

| Lesson/Start Date(s): | | Practice Goal: (MINS/DAY) | |

*SCALES, CHORDS, ARPEGGIOS, MUSIC PIECES, THEORY, PAGE NO. ETC... ✓ / Minutes / Signature etc...

CATEGORY*	NOTES	Su	Mo	Tu	We	Th	Fr	Sa

ADDITIONAL NOTES:

PRACTICE LOG

Lesson/Start Date(s): _____ *Practice Goal: (MINS/DAY)* _____

*SCALES, CHORDS, ARPEGGIOS, MUSIC PIECES, THEORY, PAGE NO. ETC... ✓ / Minutes / Signature etc...

CATEGORY*	NOTES	Su	Mo	Tu	We	Th	Fr	Sa

Lesson/Start Date(s): _____ *Practice Goal: (MINS/DAY)* _____

*SCALES, CHORDS, ARPEGGIOS, MUSIC PIECES, THEORY, PAGE NO. ETC... ✓ / Minutes / Signature etc...

CATEGORY*	NOTES	Su	Mo	Tu	We	Th	Fr	Sa

ADDITIONAL NOTES:

Made in the USA
Middletown, DE
30 November 2022